M000119889

Pebbles on the Road

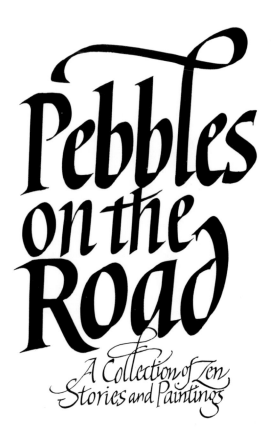

Pebbles
on the
Road

A Collection of Zen
Stories and Paintings

STEPHEN CASSETTARI

Angus&Robertson
An imprint of HarperCollins*Publishers*

AN ANGUS & ROBERTSON BOOK
An imprint of HarperCollinsPublishers

First published in Australia in 1992 by
CollinsAngus&Robertson Publishers Pty Limited (ACN 009 913 517)
A division of HarperCollinsPublishers (Australia) Pty Limited
25-31 Ryde Road, Pymble NSW 2073, Australia

HarperCollinsPublishers (New Zealand) Limited
31 View Road, Glenfield, Auckland 10, New Zealand

HarperCollinsPublishers Limited
77-85 Fulham Palace Road, London W6 8JB, United Kingdom

Distributed in the United States of America by
HarperCollinsPublishers
10 East 53rd Street, New York NY 10022, USA

National Library of Australia
Cataloguing-in-Publication data:

Cassettari, Stephen.
    Pebbles on the road: a collection of Zen stories, sayings and paintings.
    ISBN 0 207 17720 1.

    1. Parables, Buddhist. 2. Zen stories. 3. Quotations, Zen. 4. Painting, Zen.
    I. Title.

294.3927

Cover calligraphy and design by Dave Wood
Printed in Hong Kong

5 4 3 2 1
96 95 94 93 92

Dedicated to Ken McLean —
Healer, friend and exponent of the
Harmonious Way of the Spirit.

THE STORIES AND SAYINGS IN THIS BOOK ARE a combination of my original work and adaptations of traditional and contemporary sources. The sayings marked ✤ and all the paintings are my original work. The saying on the page preceding the introduction is inspired by the work of Guillaume Apollinaire. I have rewritten the traditional stories to unify the style but whatever their source they all point directly to the heart, clearing away the unessential leaving only that which *is*.

Pebbles on the road...
Dancing in the rain...
Swimming between the islands...
Skipping over the canyons...
Playing among the stars... ✦

'Go to the edge,' the voice said.
'No!' they said. 'We will fall.'
'Go to the edge,' the voice said.
'No!' they said. 'We will be pushed over.'
'Go to the edge,' the voice said.
So they went...
  and they were pushed...
    and they flew...

INTRODUCTION

PEBBLES ON THE ROAD IS A COLLECTION OF parables, sayings and paintings that portray the spontaneous immediacy of Zen.

Zen is a school of Buddhism which advocates sudden enlightenment or awareness as opposed to the more gradual evolution of the other meditative schools of Buddhism. One of its methods of conveying the essence of understanding is through the use of parables, sayings and the universal images of nature.

Zen is often used separately as a term to indicate that which is immediate. Here! Now! This is the interpretation of it in this book.

The text and illustrations are used together in this book because in the Oriental approach, words and pictures cannot be separated as they are part of each other — the words compliment the picture and the sentiment is made clear. In their simplicity the ink paintings transcend words.

To allow the reader to come to their own understanding of this book the parables included are written with open endings and the sayings can be interpreted on a variety of levels. Some can reveal deeper, even opposite meanings from their surface interpretation, presenting the essence of each event.

Thus, the anecdotes, sayings and paintings enhance each other and present a concept of awareness to be absorbed, but also leave enough unstated for the reader to arrive at their own understanding.

All the concepts in this book engender a quality of strength and hope to encourage those on the road of daily existence.

LOOKING IN THE LIGHT

A MAN CAME HOME LATE AT NIGHT. AS HE WAS approaching his gate he took the house key out of his pocket. In doing so he accidently dropped it on the ground where it was lost in the darkness.

He walked up to the door, which he found his wife had left ajar for him. He turned on the hall light and began to search around the floor, looking under the furniture for his missing key.

His wife, awakened by the light and noise, came downstairs and asked him what he was looking for. When he replied that he had lost his door key she too got down on the floor and began to search.

The man turned on the lights of the living room and continued the search. After some time of fruitless searching his wife asked him exactly where he had dropped the key. When he replied that he had lost it by the gate, she stood up and demanded to know why he was looking for it in the house. He calmly replied that it was far too dark outside and there was much more light inside the house.

A candle in the dark
seems bright
until it meets
the sunlight. ❖

Freedom is not the liberty
to do what you want.
Rather it is the ability
to do what is required.

GIVING THE MOON

A MONK SITTING ON THE VERANDAH OF HIS house was absorbed in the contemplation of the full moon. A thief entered the back of his house and began to search for valuables. The monk heard a noise and went inside to investigate. When he saw what the thief was doing he said to him, 'Let me help you,' and proceeded to load the thief up with valuables. He then showed him out the front door and once again took up his position on the verandah. Looking up at the moon he said to himself, 'I can give you everything I have but I can't give you the moon.'

Later that night some soldiers brought the thief back to the monk's house. They told the monk they had caught him in possession of the monk's goods. 'He did not steal them,' said the monk. 'I gave them to him.'

The soldiers then went away leaving the thief with the monk. The thief, amazed at the monk's generosity, sat down on the verandah beside him and looked up into the sky to see what the monk was so absorbed with.

'Now,' said the monk. 'I can give you the moon.'

Some steal my money
others steal my time.
But if I feel no remorse,
they commit no crime.

Neither giving nor taking,
nothing is gained nor lost,
offering and accepting
everything is worth the cost. ❖

SAILING ON THE RIVER

A GREAT CHINESE LANDSCAPE ARTIST SPENT many months on a large mural. Having completed the final strokes he stepped back to survey the finished work. He sighed deeply and told his apprentice that this was his greatest work and that he could never hope to do a better painting.

He handed his brush to his apprentice and walked up to the edge of the mural. He then calmly stepped onto a rock painted in the foreground of the mural and got into a boat that was moored beside it. He raised the sail and steered the boat across the lake where he rounded the headland and disappeared forever beyond the horizon.

Living on the edge
is perilous,
but the view more
than compensates. ❖

The act of painting
is like walking on water.
If you think about
what you are doing
you fall in. ❖

MAYBE

A FARMER LIVED JUST OUTSIDE A SMALL VILLAGE at the base of some hills. He had a fine son who was much admired by his neighbours. When the neighbours would compliment the farmer on his good fortune in having such a son, he would shrug his shoulders and quietly say, 'Maybe it's good fortune, maybe it's not.'

One day the farmer's stallion broke out of its field and ran off into the hills. When the neighbours came to console the farmer on his bad fortune, he simply shrugged his shoulders and said, 'Maybe it's bad fortune, maybe it's not.'

The son went to look for the stallion and found it at the head of a herd of twenty wild horses. When he led his father's stallion home the other horses followed it into the field. The neighbours came to congratulate the farmer on his good fortune at such an addition to his stock. The farmer replied, 'Maybe it is, maybe it's not.'

When the son was breaking in one of the wild horses it threw him and he landed hard on the ground and broke his leg. The neighbours came to offer their condolences to the farmer. 'How unlucky!' they said. 'Maybe,' said the farmer.

The next day a messenger from the emperor brought a decree to the village conscripting all able-bodied young men into the army. Because of his injury the farmer's son was not conscripted.

*Accept neither success
nor failure.* ❖

A circle begins anywhere. ❖

HEAVEN AND HELL

A GREAT AND POWERFUL WARRIOR CAME TO THE head monk of a monastery. He asked the monk to show him the difference between heaven and hell.

The monk sneered at the warrior and said, 'One as arrogant and small-minded as you would never be able to learn the difference between heaven and hell.' After more such abuse the warrior lost his temper and yelled, 'I will show you death then!' and began to draw his sword out of its scabbard.

The monk smiled widely and calmly said, 'That is hell.' The warrior at once understood and pushed his sword back down into its scabbard.

Again, the monk smiled and said, 'And that is heaven.'

If you climb
on a tiger's back
the difficulty
is in getting off again.

A long journey reveals
the strength of a horse.

HERE ALL THE TIME

A MOTHER AND HER YOUNG SON WENT TO THE busy market place and became separated. After frantically searching for her son throughout the market his mother finally found him playing beside a stall that sold toys.

'Weren't you worried when you got lost?' cried his mother. The boy replied, 'I was not lost, I was here all the time.'

Never hope—
and do not worry.

When you see
a man drowning
you do not wait
until he calls for help
before you rescue him.
Though it is advisable—
to ensure that he is
not merely waving
to a friend.

THE OBSTACLE

A T THE END OF A HARD DAY'S WORK, A FARMER left his hillside field and began descending the narrow, winding path to his home. He carried his spade and hoe and his dog followed him.

Along the path the farmer found that a fallen rock was blocking his way. Tired and hungry, with dusk approaching, he began digging at the base of the rock to attempt to move it. After much struggle he still couldn't move it and he felt even more tired.

The dog, having wandered away, came back and barked at the farmer. The dog tried to lead the farmer away from the rock, but he was determined not to be distracted from his objective and continued in his struggle.

Again the dog tried to get the farmer's attention but the farmer ignored him. Because it was getting dark the farmer decided to stay where he was and sleep in the hollow he had dug.

Upon awakening in the early morning light, he heard his dog barking further along the path, beyond the rock. After taking a few steps back from the rock the farmer could see that, having been so close to the rock in his efforts to move it, he had not noticed that the fall of the rock had made a rough passage to a lower section of the path.

The water is not impeded
 by the rock,
but flows effortlessly
 round it,
   wearing it away with time. ❖

The falling rock is not deflected
 from its path,
but parts the water,
leaving it to continue
   on its own journey. ❖

THE ROSE AND THE OAK

AN OAK TREE GREW IN A GARDEN FOR MORE than forty years. One summer a nearby rosebud began to unfold the glorious colours of its petals.

The oak tree was tired of being the same dull shades of green and brown and longed to be as beautiful as the rose. One morning, when the rose was in its full glory, the tree told the rose of its desire to be like it. The rose in turn expressed its admiration for the height and strength of the oak tree and told the tree that it would be most willing to change places for a day. And so with the aid of the garden spirits, they did.

That afternoon a gardener came and cut the rose to take into the house.

After the rain ~
Everything grows
more beautiful.

Flowers do not explain
their beauty.
The storm gives no reason
for its anger. ❖

THE DRAGON'S EYES

A MASTER ARTIST WAS REQUESTED TO APPEAR AT the emperor's palace to paint a dragon mural for the emperor. He replied that he was too busy on more important work and he would not be able to paint the mural.

The emperor's secretary called on the master artist with a royal command for the artist to appear at the palace to paint the mural. Again the artist replied that he was too busy.

The emperor's personal guard came and took the artist by force to the palace and told him he must paint the mural or be executed. The artist proceeded to paint a most magnificent dragon of blue and green, embellished with gold. He worked without stopping and finished the mural in a single day.

The emperor's secretary came to view the completed mural and declared it a great work of art. He paid the artist the amount of gold decreed by the emperor and said that the emperor would view the mural with the court the following morning.

The artist stayed to put the finishing touches on the mural. When all the palace was asleep he mixed white paint with ground pearl and placed a small dot in the centre of each of the dragon's eyes. Gathering up his paints and brushes he then departed for the distant mountains.

The next morning the mural was unveiled before the assembled court. Just as praise was being given for the life-like quality of the work the dragon's eyes blinked. The dragon then turned his head around, stretched his wings and flew out of a palace window, leaving a blank wall that bore only the red seal of the artist.

I walk among beggars and kings
without being noticed.
But I don't mind,
it leaves more time
for sunsets and children. ❖

A shadow has no shadow.

LESS AND LESS

THERE WAS A FARMER WHO WAS ALWAYS looking for ways to save his money. He sold his horse to buy a smaller, less expensive donkey, making it do the same amount of work. He also decided to save even more money by feeding it less.

He reduced the bale of hay he fed the donkey by a handful each day. It was so little, that he thought the donkey would not notice. Eventually, the donkey was performing the same amount of work on less than a quarter of a bale of hay and the farmer was very pleased with himself.

The farmer was very surprised and most upset when one morning the donkey was found dead in its stall.

One stone at a time.

You can't step
in the same river twice.

TWO MONKS

TWO MONKS WERE WALKING BACK TO THEIR monastery when they came to a ford at a stream. At the ford a pretty farmer's daughter asked them to help her to cross the stream as she did not want to get mud on her new dress.

The first monk ignored her and continued on his way remembering the strict rules of their order not even to look at women. Without speaking the second monk picked her up in his arms and carried her across the stream. He let her down on the other side and continued walking with the other monk.

The first monk began to chastise him, asking him if he had forgotten about the strict rules of their order. He kept referring to the incident all the way back to the monastery.

As they reached the gateway of the monastery he referred to the matter again. The second monk turned to him and said, 'Are you still carrying the woman with you? I left her at the stream.'

When you have finished
eating your rice,
wash out your bowl.

The illusion of choice
leaves only disappointment.
The joy of acceptance
offers understanding. ❖

STOP CRYING

A MAN OF LEARNING CAME TO THE HEAD MONK of a monastery to ask about the nature of the monastery's teaching.

He asked the head monk many questions, which were in fact statements of what the man believed the teachings were about. To all his statements the head monk listened calmly, gently nodding his head and replying, 'Yes, that is so.'

Finally the man said, 'Then you have nothing to tell me as I already know what you teach.'

'Oh no,' replied the monk. 'The teachings are nothing like you believe them to be.'

'Then why have you been agreeing with me?' demanded the man.

The monk smiled kindly and replied, 'Before you can feed the baby you must stop it crying.'

Before an action,
hesitate.
During the action
do not hesitate.

Emptiness is full
of potential. ❖

THE TRUE STUDENT

A LEARNED MONK HAD MANY STUDENTS WHO lived in a temple with him. One student used to steal from the others. After many appeals to their master to reprimand this student, the other students presented themselves before the master with the ultimatum that either he dismissed the thief or they would leave.

The master bowed and replied, 'Then you must go, for you are all good students and will easily find another to teach you but this thief is irredeemable and if I throw him out he will find no-one else to care for him.'

Do not confuse truth
with sincerity.

Mountains are higher
than rivers.
But each follows
its own course
under the sky. ❖

THE FULL CUP

AN ARROGANT BUSINESS MAN CAME TO A monastery and said to the head monk, 'I have learnt much of the material world in my life so far. Now I wish to learn of spiritual knowledge.'

The monk said, 'Maybe you will get the opportunity but first let us have a cup of tea while we discuss the matter.'

After making the tea the monk poured some into a cup, set for the business man. When the level of the tea reached the top of the cup the monk kept on pouring and it overflowed onto the clothes of the business man. He jumped up and exclaimed, 'What are you doing?'

The monk replied, 'You are like the cup, so full that there is no room to put in any more. First you must empty yourself.'

You have begun
once the intention
is there.

All you need to be rich
is treasure in your heart. ❖

THE THREE BROTHERS

A RICH MAN WAS DYING SO HE CALLED HIS three sons and said to them, 'I wish to leave my fortune intact so I will set each of you the same task to see which one is the most capable at managing money.

'In my warehouse there are three large store-rooms, all of the same size. Here is a bag of silver each. Your task is to each fill one storeroom with as much as your silver will buy.'

The first son bought sand with all his money and filled a third of his room.

The second son bought soil with all his money and filled half his room.

The third son spent only a small portion of his money and bought some candles and matches to fill his room with light.

Quality
rather than quantity.

Intuition is spontaneous knowledge
gained through experience. ❖

THE IMAGE OF THE DRAGON

THE IMAGE OF THE DRAGON IS OFTEN SEEN IN the expressions of nature; in the vapours of clouds, the flowing of water or fire, twisted tree trunks and eccentrically shaped rocks.

The Chinese dragon has no wings and breathes no fire; it swims through the air by the undulations of its body like an eel in water. It produces fire by the friction of its body movement against the air.

It is an auspicious symbol, bringing good luck to those who see it, clearing away illusion and revealing truth.

The depiction of the five-clawed dragon was the prerogative of the emperor. The four-clawed dragon was for lesser officials and the three-clawed variety for more common use.

The dragon consists of the head of a horse, the horns of a deer, the mane of a lion, the body of a snake and the feet of an eagle.

Being large one has
  respect for the small.
Being old one has
  sympathy with the young. ❖

Cherish carefully
  the friendship of nature.
Let her gracious blessings
  fill your quiet moments.

TRADITIONAL CONCEPTS OF COLOUR IN DRAGON REPRESENTATION

Black Dragon
North – Winter
Water – Death

White Dragon
West – Autumn
Rock – Age

Yellow Dragon
– Centre –
Earth – Harmony

Green Dragon
East – Spring
Trees – Birth

Red Dragon
South – Summer
Fire – Youth

THIS IS THE SYMBOL OF TAI CHI WHICH IS USED HERE TO display the traditional concepts of colour in dragon representation. Tai Chi means 'the grand ultimate' and symbolises the harmonious unity of complementary opposites (the Yin Yang), each of which contains the other. Together they are a whole unit that is greater than the combined parts. Not only is the symbol repeated on a diminishing scale within each section but it is itself, one 'eye' of a larger symbol. Thus, the overall concept is not circular but rather that of an infinite spiral.

龍

Zen symbol for dragon

EXERCISES IN BEING

Think — Understand.

Wait — Passively alert.

Eat — According to need.

Look at the stars.

Talk to a rock.

Hug a tree.

Listen to the rain.

When in company
act as if alone.

When alone act as if
in company.

Spend one day without speaking.

Spend one hour with eyes closed.

With eyes closed,
have someone you are close to
take you on a walk.

Think of something to say
to someone particular.
Next time you see them,
don't say it.

Go somewhere particular
to do something.
When you get there
don't do it.

Walk backwards.

Upon awakening
immediately get up.

Get dressed to go somewhere
then don't go.

Just go out immediately
as you are, anywhere.

Do what comes next.

Walk on ! *

SEEING THE LIGHT

LIGHT A CANDLE,
observe the flame.
Close your eyes,
and still see the flame.
Watch as it slowly fades.
Look at the flame again.
Light another candle
from the first flame.
Nothing is taken away
from the first flame
in the act of giving
life to another flame.
Let the two flames
merge together.
Is there one flame or two?
Blow out the flame.
Where did it return to?
With eyes closed
see the image of the flame.
Blow that out too.
What is left . . . ? ❖